I0797524

DRONES

Military Drones

BY CECILIA PINTO MCCARTHY

CONTENT CONSULTANT
MICHAEL BRAASCH, PHD, PE
THOMAS PROFESSOR OF ELECTRICAL ENGINEERING
OHIO UNIVERSITY

Kids Core
An Imprint of Abdo Publishing
abdobooks.com

abdobooks.com

Printed in the United States of America, North Mankato, Minnesota
082020
012021

Cover Photo: Airman 1st Class William Rio Rosado/Defense Visual Information Distribution Service
Interior Photos: Isaac Brekken/Getty Images News/Getty Images, 4–5, 28; Senior Airman Haley Stevens/Defense Visual Information Distribution Service, 7; Airman 1st Class William Rio Rosado/Defense Visual Information Distribution Service, 9; Cpl. Ricky S. Gomez/US Marine Corps/Defense Visual Information Distribution Service, 10; US Air Force Photo/Alamy, 12–13, 29 (top); Senior Airman Juan Torres/Defense Visual Information Distribution Service, 14; Sgt. Brittany Johnson/Defense Visual Information Distribution Service, 16; Bob Edme/AP Images, 19; Ben Stansall/AFP/Getty Images, 20, 29 (bottom); Senior Airman Joshua Hoskins/US Air Force, 22–23; Petty Officer 2nd Class Anderson W Branch/Defense Visual Information Distribution Service, 25; Pvt. James Newsome/Defense Visual Information Distribution Service, 27

Editor: Maddie Spalding
Series Designer: Katharine Hale

Library of Congress Control Number: 2019954183

Publisher's Cataloging-in-Publication Data

Names: McCarthy, Cecilia Pinto, author
Title: Military drones / by Cecilia Pinto McCarthy
Description: Minneapolis, Minnesota : Abdo Publishing, 2021 | Series: Drones | Includes online resources and index.
Identifiers: ISBN 9781532192791 (lib. bdg.) | ISBN 9781644944394 (pbk.) | ISBN 9781098210694 (ebook)
Subjects: LCSH: Drone aircraft--Juvenile literature. | Combat drone aircraft--Juvenile literature. | UCAVs (Military science)--Juvenile literature. | Uninhabited combat aerial vehicles--Juvenile literature. | Military Robots--Juvenile literature.
Classification: DDC 623.7469--dc23

CONTENTS

The MQ-9 Reaper drone can fly up to 50,000 feet (15,200 m) above the earth.

CHAPTER 1

A Direct Hit

In 2017, an MQ-9 Reaper drone took off from Creech Air Force Base in Nevada. It was on a test mission. A pilot and a **sensor** operator sat in a ground control station (GCS). The pilot controlled the drone's speed and direction.

The sensor operator controlled the drone's cameras. The cameras recorded what was around and below the drone. The pilot and sensor operator watched the live video on screens. They were searching for the target drone.

The team found the other drone. The sensor operator fired a **missile** from the Reaper. A direct hit! The target drone exploded. This was the first time a flying drone had shot down another drone in midair.

Control from Afar

A drone sometimes flies near a GCS. But officers can also fly a drone from thousands of miles away. US Air Force pilots at a GCS in Syracuse, New York, often fly drones in the Middle East.

It takes a team of people to maintain and repair an MQ-9 Reaper drone.

What Are Drones?

The Reaper is a military drone. Drones are special aircraft or ships. There are no pilots on board. People control drones from the ground. Drones that fly are also called unmanned **aerial** vehicles (UAVs).

Drones have computers. Operators use satellite signals to communicate with these computers. Satellites are machines in space. They send signals back and forth between drones and control stations. But some drones communicate directly with soldiers on the ground. They do not need satellites.

Drone Uses

The US military uses drones for special missions. These drones have cameras and other tools. With these tools, drones can gather information. They can spy on enemies. Then officers can warn troops about dangers. Drones can also find and fire upon enemy targets.

Diagram of a Reaper Drone

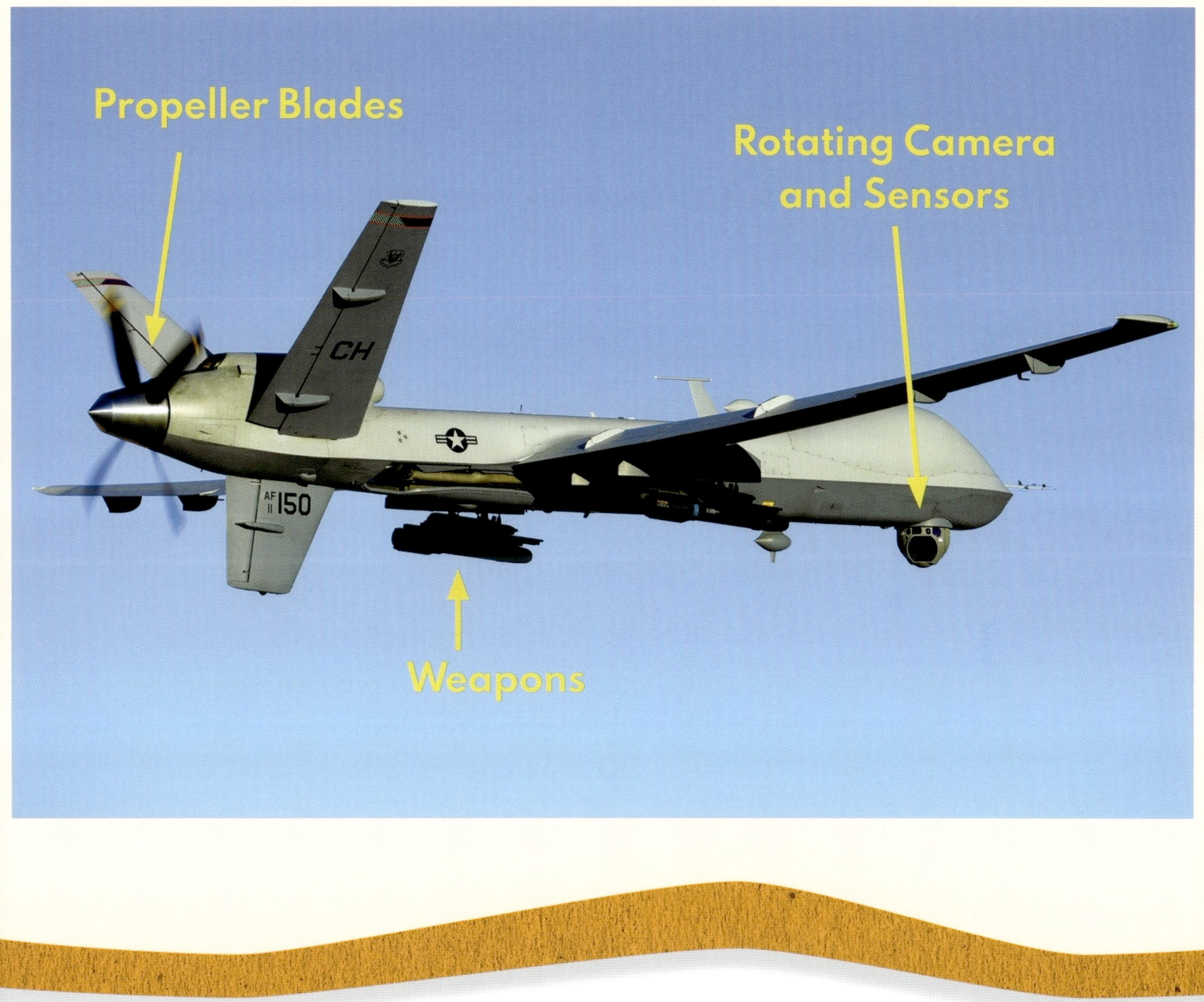

This diagram shows the parts of a Reaper drone. The spinning propeller blades lift the drone. Other parts of the drone are helpful for many types of military missions.

The US Army uses the RQ-7B Shadow drone to survey areas and spy on enemies.

Military drones can save lives too. Drone cameras can find wounded soldiers and aircraft that have been shot down. Military drones are also useful in noncombat situations. During natural disasters, such as hurricanes, they can help with search and rescue missions. Drones can find stranded or injured people.

Primary Source

Reaper drones have many uses. Lieutenant Colonel Micaela Brancato explains:

> The American people need to understand that the Reaper . . . really can help, whether it's disaster [relief] or search and rescue.

Source: Technical Sergeant Gregory Solman. "Air Force Drones Help California Firefighters Combat Wildfires." *US Department of Defense*, 19 Oct. 2017, defense.gov. Accessed 29 Sept. 2019.

Point of View

What is Brancato's point of view about Reaper drones? What is your point of view? Write a short essay about how these views are similar and different.

RQ-4 Global Hawk drones can stay in the air for more than 30 hours at a time.

CHAPTER 2

Spies in the Sky

Military drones come in many shapes and sizes. Some are large. The RQ-4 Global Hawk drone has a wingspan of 130 feet (40 m). It can fly more than 11 miles (18 km) above the earth. That's twice as high as a passenger plane flies.

Global Hawks are used on US Air Force bases around the world.

The US Air Force and US Navy use Global Hawks. These drones scan water and coastlines for enemies. They follow flight routes

programmed in their computers. They can take off, fly, and land by themselves.

Special Equipment

A Global Hawk's cameras work day and night. Some cameras can find objects in the dark. The cameras sense the heat given off by the objects.

Disaster Relief

In November 2013, Typhoon Haiyan hit the Philippines. The storm destroyed roads and airports. Many people were stranded. The US military sent a Global Hawk to the area. The drone's cameras showed the roads and airports that were not damaged. Rescue teams quickly found the routes they could take to reach people.

Operators at a GCS use special equipment to control a drone's speed, direction, and altitude.

Different temperatures appear as different colors. The colors show up on a screen at a GCS. Officers at the GCS review the images to find enemy forces and structures. The cameras can detect people and buildings. They can also show enemy vehicles and weapons.

The Global Hawk also has **radar**. Radar uses **radio waves** to find objects. An antenna on the drone sends out radio waves. The waves travel until they hit an object. Then they bounce back to a receiver on the drone. The receiver can determine the location, size, and speed of the object. GCS operators see the object on a screen. They can track moving ships and other vehicles.

Microdrones

Another type of military drone is a microdrone. Microdrones are pocket-sized UAVs. The Black Hornet is a microdrone. It has spinning blades like a helicopter. The blades allow it to fly and hover. A Black Hornet can travel up to 13 miles per hour (21 km/h). It can keep up this speed for about 25 minutes. Then its battery needs to be recharged.

To fly a Black Hornet, a soldier presses buttons on a controller. Soldiers can also program the drone to follow a route. Then the drone will fly on its own.

A Black Hornet drone is 6 inches (15 cm) long. This makes it about the length of a pencil.

A Black Hornet drone makes almost no noise as it moves through the air.

Small and Stealthy

Troops use Black Hornets to scan unknown areas. The drone's cameras send back images and live video. Soldiers see the images and video on a handheld display screen. Black Hornets can zip into dark buildings and caves. They can even travel inside pipes to find hidden bombs. Knowing what lies ahead can help keep troops safe.

Explore Online

Visit the website below. Did you learn any new information about the Global Hawk that wasn't in Chapter Two?

RQ-4: Defining the Team

abdocorelibrary.com/military-drones

The XQ-58A Valkyrie drone's top speed is 652 miles per hour (1,050 km/h).

CHAPTER 3

New and Future Drones

In 2019, the US Air Force began test-flying a UAV called the XQ-58A Valkyrie. The air force plans to use Valkyries alongside fighter jets. These drones could carry weapons and fire at enemy targets. They could also be used in place of some fighter jets.

Jets that are damaged or destroyed cost a lot to replace. Valkyries cost less to build. Using Valkyries could also mean fewer pilots in the air. Fewer pilots mean fewer injuries and deaths.

The Knifefish

The US military also uses underwater drones. This type of drone is often called an unmanned

Gremlins

Gremlins are small UAVs. They are shaped like missiles. Pilots load them onto military aircraft. Then they are launched. Gremlins communicate with each other. They work together as a group. Their cameras and sensors gather information about enemy forces. When they finish their job, Gremlins return to the larger plane.

The Knifefish drone weighs about 2,030 pounds (920 kg). Workers need to use a crane to move it.

underwater vehicle (UUV). The US Navy created a UUV called the Knifefish. This drone has **sonar** equipment. Sonar uses sound waves. The drone makes a sound. The sound travels in waves until it hits an object. The navy uses the Knifefish to find underwater mines. The drone can also identify the type of mine. This helps experts figure out how to safely get rid of the mine.

Artificial Intelligence

The US military hopes that Valkyries and other future drones will have artificial intelligence (AI). AI is a type of computer science. It helps machines understand and solve problems. Drones with AI would be able to learn new skills. They could complete missions on their own.

Today's researchers are designing drones that will be smaller, quieter, and faster than modern drones. The US military wants to create UAVs that can stay in the air for longer periods of time. In the future, military drones may be able to do more jobs.

The US military also uses swarm drones. Swarm drones can work together to complete military missions.

Further Evidence

Look at the website below. Does it give any new evidence to support the information in Chapter Three?

Drones to the Rescue

abdocorelibrary.com/military-drones

Drone Stats

MQ-9 Reaper

- Controlled remotely from a GCS
- Has cameras and sensor equipment
- Can fire missiles

RQ-4 Global Hawk

- Used primarily to spy on enemies
- Has special cameras to see people and objects in the dark
- Can fly more than 11 miles (18 km) above the earth

Black Hornet

- Microdrone
- Used to gather information about unknown places
- Can go in small spaces where soldiers cannot fit

Glossary

aerial
describing something that happens in or involves the air

missile
a weapon carried by a rocket that can hit faraway objects

programmed
entered instructions into a computer to tell it what to do

radar
a machine that uses radio waves to find the position of objects

radio waves
waves that are used to send information over distances to radios, televisions, and other devices

sensor
a type of equipment that can detect things such as heat, light, sound, or pressure

sonar
a device that sends out sound waves to find objects underwater

Online Resources

To learn more about military drones, visit our free resource websites below.

Visit **abdocorelibrary.com** or scan this QR code for free Common Core resources for teachers and students, including vetted activities, multimedia, and booklinks, for deeper subject comprehension.

Visit **abdobooklinks.com** or scan this QR code for free additional online weblinks for further learning. These links are routinely monitored and updated to provide the most current information available.

Learn More

Abell, Tracy, and Alexis Roumanis. *Drones*. AV2 by Weigl, 2019.

Bassier, Emma. *Military Vehicles*. Abdo Publishing, 2020.

Olson, Elsie. *Drones*. Abdo Publishing, 2018.

Index

About the Author

Cecilia Pinto McCarthy has written more than 30 books for young readers. She and her family live north of Boston, Massachusetts.